The Lord's Supper

D1462823

The Lord's Supper

Peter Jeffery

 EVANGELICAL PRESS

EVANGELICAL PRESS
Grange Close, Faverdale North Industrial Estate, Darlington,
Co. Durham, DL3 0PH, England

First published 1997

British Library Cataloguing in Publication Data available

ISBN 0 85234 402 3

Printed and bound by Creative Print and Design, Ebbw Vale, Wales.

Contents

Foreword

Ignorance is always a great enemy of true Christianity. An untaught believer will drift through the outward forms of Christian worship unaware of their true meaning. Perhaps it would be more accurate to say that, having a very dim light, he stumbles along the Christian pathway. Understanding is essential to profitable devotion and to sure-footed pilgrimage towards the heavenly Jerusalem.

There is nothing in the secular world to prepare a young convert to Christ to comprehend the meaning of the Lord's Supper. Yet entering a body of saints he is repeatedly confronted with this coming to the table. And it is attended with a condemnation of failing to have 'discernment' while one participates! (1 Cor. 11:29).

Peter Jeffery gives important and wise pastoral assistance to those who are young in the faith. This book on 'the Lord's Supper' may serve as a primer explaining language necessarily used repeatedly in this special ceremony of worship. He touches on important questions that many will ask, pointing to balanced and biblical answers which avoid unfortunate extremes of practice into which some have fallen.

Since your Lord Jesus has commanded you to worship him at his table, and since he expects you to do so with a discerning heart, Mr Jeffery's book should be a fine aid for you to 'grow in the grace and knowledge of our Lord and Saviour Jesus Christ' (2 Peter 3:18).

What a magnificent privilege it is to be a partaker of the Lord Jesus Christ! What delights Christians have discovered as they sup with Christ! May a firm grasp of the meaning of the supper lead you into deeper joys in your Lord.

Walter J. Chantry

1.
The Lord's Supper

'I received from the Lord what I also passed on to you'
(1 Cor. 11:23).

The Lord's Supper is a gathering of the Lord's people in which they obey the command of the Lord Jesus Christ to celebrate his atoning death and the salvation it affords to those who trust in him. This service is thus one of:

1. Remembrance of Christ;
2. Obedience to Christ;
3. Worship of Christ;
4. Fellowship with Christ and with his people.

In the course of this celebration certain symbols are used, namely bread, which is broken to symbolize Christ's body 'broken' on the cross, and wine, which is poured out to symbolize his blood shed for our sins. Furthermore, these symbols are consumed by those present to represent their personal participation in the saving work of Christ.

The first supper

On the night before he was to die on the cross, Jesus met with his apostles to eat the Passover meal. This was not an accidental occurrence determined by the time of the year, but an essential part of God's eternal plan. Throughout the Gospels we find Jesus telling the apostles that his time had not yet come. He was referring to the time when he was to die for the sins of his people. It was not mere circumstance that set this time, but God himself, and the time in question was to be the Feast of Passover.

The reason for this is clearly expressed by Paul in 1 Corinthians 5:7, where he tells us, 'Christ, our Passover lamb, has been sacrificed.' The apostle is saying that the Old Testament event of the Passover, when God spared his people from judgement and delivered them from bondage in Egypt, was a God-given picture of the meaning of the death of Christ. At the first Passover a lamb, which had to be without any blemish or defect, was sacrificed in every Jewish home, and its blood sprinkled on the door-posts and lintels of those homes. When the destroying angel passed through Egypt that night in judgement, killing all the first-born in the land, he passed over those houses where he saw the blood, and their children alone were spared. In effect, the lamb had died as a substitute for the Jewish first-born. In like manner, Jesus is the Lamb of God who shed his blood to deliver us from God's death-penalty upon sin.

The first celebration of the Lord's Supper, therefore, took place in the context of the Passover meal. Tradition calls it 'the Last Supper', but in truth it was the first! At the table Jesus said to his disciples, 'I have eagerly desired to eat this Passover with you before I suffer' (Luke 22:15). At any Passover meal the people would eat from three cakes of unleavened bread and drink from four cups of wine. Jesus used these things, which were well known to his friends, as symbols of the meaning of his impending death.

The name

The institution of the Lord's Supper is recorded in Matthew 26:17-30; Mark 14:12-26 and Luke 22:7-23, but the fullest account is given by the apostle Paul in 1 Corinthians 11, and we shall be concentrating on this portion of Scripture in this book. In this passage Paul calls the service 'the Lord's Supper' (v. 20), but this is not the only term used in the New Testament to describe it. It is called communion (1 Cor. 10:16, NKJV), the breaking of bread (Acts 2:42) and the Lord's Table (1 Cor. 10:21). So we may use any of these names and be perfectly biblical. Later in church history it was called the Eucharist. Although this word simply means 'thanksgiving', it has been adopted by those churches which teach, wrongly, that the bread and the wine in some way become the body and blood of Christ. It is therefore a term which evangelicals avoid.

The various names used to describe this service are significant. 'The Lord's Table' speaks of grace — that is, God's free, abundant giving. It tells us, as it were, of the hospitality of God towards undeserving sinners. The psalmist uses this imagery in Psalm 23. As the much-loved paraphrase puts it:

Thou spread'st a table in my sight,
Thy unction grace bestoweth,
And Oh, what transport of delight,
From thy pure chalice floweth![1]

The same picture of overflowing hospitality is used in the parable of the great feast in Luke 14:16-24. It was the 'the poor, the crippled, the blind and the lame' who sat down before the sumptuous meal prepared by the master. So it is with Christ, for he did 'not come to call the righteous, but sinners to repentance' (Luke 5:32), and what a feast of love and mercy he provides for those who trust in him! We shall consider the centrality of grace more fully when we come to the subject of the new covenant, but suffice it to say here that the Lord's Table speaks to us of the superabundance of God's provision in Christ for undeserving sinners such as ourselves.

The terms 'communion' and 'supper' have a slightly different connotation. They relate to fellowship and intimacy with Christ. Thus the Lord's Table is an occasion when we ought to enjoy a special closeness to the Lord. It was to the spiritually impoverished church at Laodicea that Jesus extended his invitation: 'Here I am! I stand at the door and knock. If anyone hears my voice and opens the door, I will come in and eat with him, and he with me' (Rev. 3:20). As with the Lord's Table, there is a meal to be enjoyed, but the emphasis here is upon the fellowship with Christ that these people were sorely missing. Coldness and spiritual poverty often afflict the church today, as was the case at Laodicea. The Lord's Supper presents us with an opportunity to restore our communion with Christ and to renew the warm intimacy with him that ought to characterize the believer's daily experience.

The picture of dining together with Christ ought also to remind us that the Lord's Table is not some ritualistic observance to be hurried through by rote. Too often its celebration is a brief afterthought, tacked on to the end of another service and treated with scant respect. It should be a time when we linger with the Lord in the enjoyment of his gracious provision for our spiritual needs.

Finally, the 'breaking of bread' is a descriptive title with a double meaning. It refers directly to Christ's death upon the cross, where his body was 'broken' for our redemption. But it also reminds us that he is the 'bread of life', the 'bread of God ... who comes down from heaven and gives life to the world' (John 6:35,33). In other words, the Lord Jesus Christ is the source of all spiritual life and sustenance. As Peter cried, 'Lord, to whom [else] shall we go? You have the words of eternal life' (John 6:68). Thus the Lord's Table reminds us also of the fact that we are utterly dependent upon Christ for salvation and preservation, for blessing in this life and glory in the next.

Sacrament and ordinance

There are two other words often used in connection with this service, namely 'sacrament' and 'ordinance'. Neither is used in Scripture in the context of the Lord's Supper (indeed, 'sacrament' is not a biblical term at all), but both convey a meaning which is biblical. The word 'ordinance' simply means that our Lord *ordained* that his followers should observe the Lord's Supper. With regard to 'sacrament', John Calvin defined it as 'an outward sign by which the Lord seals on our conscience the promises of his goodwill towards us in order to sustain the weakness of our faith; and we in turn attest our piety towards him in the presence of the Lord and of his angels and before men'.[2]

Although the term 'sacrament' is used in Roman Catholicism to describe a variety of rituals, evangelical Christians point out that there are four elements that constitute and characterize a genuine biblical sacrament:

1. The sacrament is a divine ordinance instituted by Christ himself.

2. The sacrament uses material elements only as visible symbols of God's blessing.

3. The sacrament is a means of grace to the one who rightly partakes of it.

4. The sacrament is a confirmation and assurance to us of the grace it signifies.[3]

Following this, most Protestant churches conclude that there are only two genuine sacraments — baptism and the Lord's Supper. Baptism is a once-and-for-all sacrament that employs water and signifies our identification with Christ in his death and resurrection. The Lord's Supper is a continuing sacrament that uses bread and wine to symbolize the body and blood of Christ and thus the believer's participation in his death and its eternal benefits. The name of this sacrament may vary, but its significance and message should not.

Received from the Lord

Paul's teaching on this sacrament in 1 Corinthians 11 is not merely his personal opinion. Neither is it something he has just inferred from the historical narrative. He is not telling the Corinthians, 'I don't like the way you are doing things and you should do it my way.' On the contrary, he is passing on teaching which is far more authoritative than a man's opinion, for he writes, 'I received *from the Lord* what I also passed on to you' (1 Cor. 11:23, emphasis added). What he was telling the Corinthians about the Lord's Table had come to him by direct revelation from Christ himself. Notice also that he had previously told them these things. Clearly, they had forgotten and needed to be reminded. It never hurts to repeat Christ's teachings and bring them forcibly to mind. Indeed, it can save us a great deal of trouble.

The apostle's first purpose in 1 Corinthians 11 is to remind us what the Lord Jesus actually did at the first communion service. So he sets the teaching in the context of 'the night he was betrayed' (1 Cor. 11:23). This reference to betrayal could not have been accidental. Paul was making a point. He seems to imply that what was happening at the Lord's Supper at Corinth was a betrayal of the spirit of love and humility that so characterized the Saviour. We too need to beware of coming to the Lord's Table with attitudes that betray Christ. As we contemplate the love of God in Christ, dying for our sins on the cross, we must put away any spirit of superiority, criticism of others, censoriousness, unkindness, harshness, backbiting, jealousy and all the other sins of attitude which plague the human heart. There is no place for such things at the foot of the cross.

We are next shown the attitude which was uppermost in Christ's own mind, as he inaugurated this sacrament —

he gave thanks. His thanksgiving was not for the bread as a source of material nourishment for his bodily needs, but for the bread as a symbol of the atoning sacrifice that was to take place the following day. At that moment when all the powers of hell were gathering against Jesus, as he faced the agonies of Gethsemane and then the cross itself, he gave thanks! There was no rebellion against the will of God and no complaining about the suffering to be endured; only thankfulness to the Father for his great grace and mercy towards undeserving sinners. Jesus gave thanks for his own impending suffering and death! The writer to the Hebrews tells us that 'For the joy set before him [he] endured the cross, scorning its shame, and sat down at the right hand of the throne of God' (Heb. 12:2).

There was in our Saviour a great commitment to do God's will. This example of Christ is of tremendous importance to us as we come to the Lord's Table. Our central thought should be of thanks and praise to God, who loved us so much that he gave his Son to die for us. We thank God for the substitutionary death of Jesus on the cross. We praise him that Christ's body was broken, and his blood shed, to save us from the consequences of our own sin. There is no room for pride here, only the grateful thanks of sinners, who deserved nothing, but received instead the grace of God in Christ. Jesus gave thanks, and so too should we.

The danger of abuse

We might assume that any gathering of Christians for worship would be good and beneficial to the church — certainly when they meet for the Lord's Supper. But, sadly, that is not necessarily so. In introducing his teaching on the Lord's Supper in 1 Corinthians 11:17, Paul says that the meetings of the Corinthian church were doing more harm than good. This is a devastating criticism but perfectly justified, as the apostle demonstrates in verses 17-22 of this chapter. Paul's answer to this situation was to expound the true meaning of the sacrament. If we are to avoid the mistakes and the sins that were associated with this special service at Corinth, we must understand what Paul teaches here.

Even when there are no problems such as Paul addressed at Corinth, our enjoyment of the Lord's Table can be spoilt. This happens when we fail to understand what we are doing or why we are doing it. The purpose of this short book is to set out in simple terms what the Lord's Supper is all about. As we understand its meaning and purpose more fully, we shall both honour the Lord and be blessed ourselves.

To take the Lord's Supper is a great privilege. At Corinth this privilege was being abused. It was their custom that before they celebrated the Lord's Supper the church gathered together for what was called a 'love feast'. This was a social gathering to which everyone brought their own food and drink, and it was probably intended to be a time of fellowship. There was nothing wrong with this, of course. But at Corinth what should have been fellowship in Christ had degenerated into a demonstration of pride and selfishness. The wealthy were flaunting their possessions at these love feasts. They would bring sumptuous meals and an abundance of drink. This was not shared with the poorer members of the congregation, but consumed blatantly, in such a way as to humiliate the less fortunate (1 Cor. 11:20-22). A sort of spiritual snobbery was being practised based on financial privilege. The whole thing was obviously wrong — particularly so because they went straight from this so-called 'love feast' to the Lord's Table.

We must learn from their mistakes. In any church there will be people who are better off financially than others. A church that consists only of wealthy people, or poor people, or well-educated people, or illiterate people, is missing out on one of the great blessings and privileges of being a church — namely, the experience of oneness in Christ in spite of very different backgrounds. Wealth, education, political leanings or ethnic background are not the basis on which Christians gather together. What unites believers is that we are all sinners saved by the grace of God in Christ.

Carelessness and superstition

We may not suffer from the one-upmanship that marred the church at Corinth, but there are other abuses which are common today. Firstly, we may come carelessly to the Lord's Table. It is amazing how thoughtless and unprepared we can be when we come to this service. How often have you gone to church and not even known that the sacrament was to be taken until you saw the table prepared at the front of the church? How often do we view the Lord's Table as an optional extra?

When I advocate 'preparation' for the service I am not thinking of any kind of ritualistic preparation, but of the preparation of the heart. We have, after all, come to remember with affection and devotion the supreme sacrifice that Christ made for us, to realize the awfulness of his death under the wrath of God and the power of his life to raise us from our own spiritual death. With these vast and majestic themes upon our minds, how can we come lightly to this feast?

At the other extreme, however, many Christians view this service with a sort of superstitious awe, as if it is somehow more spiritual or mystical than other services. This is a legacy of Roman Catholicism and other ritualistic churches, which teach that Christ is present in some special way at the communion service. It is a legacy we can do without.

Dr Ernest Kevan wrote with great perception, 'The Lord's Supper is a special means of grace, but not a means of special grace. In other words, there is nothing we receive in the Lord's Supper which we do not receive when we are on our knees at home seeking the face of the Lord, or sitting in the pew listening to the preaching from the pulpit. We receive nothing different. The blessing is coming to us through another channel, that is all.'[4]

Whatever the nature of the abuse, there is but one way to guard against it. That is to make sure that we understand the true nature of the communion service and what it really means. The greater our understanding, the less likely we shall be to misuse the sacrament and its symbols, and the more likely we shall be to derive from them the blessing and comfort that the Lord intends. To promote that understanding is the chief purpose of this book.

2.
The new covenant

'After supper he took the cup, saying, "This cup is the new covenant in my blood"' (1 Cor. 11:25).

At the heart of the communion service, or Lord's Supper, stands a profound reality, namely, the new covenant. We have this on the authority of Christ himself. At the Passover meal that preceded his betrayal, he handed the wine-cup to his disciples and said, 'This cup is the new covenant in my blood' (1 Cor. 11:25). What did he mean, and what does it signify for us? These are important questions and we shall try to answer them in this chapter.

What is a covenant?

The first thing we must consider is what the Bible means by a covenant. A covenant is normally a contract between two equal parties, but this is not necessarily the case. A covenant can take the form of a testament in which, although there are still two parties, the testator and the beneficiary, the terms are set by the testator alone. The word 'covenant', then, is used in Scripture with the same flexibility as in our own day and language. We need to distinguish two separate cases.

Firstly, there is the eternal covenant made between God the Father and God the Son. This is sometimes called 'the covenant of redemption'. In this covenant the Father gave to the Son, and the Son undertook to redeem, a people chosen out of all mankind on the sole grounds of God's free grace and mercy. Of this covenant Dr Kevan writes, 'In the New Testament covenant of grace there are not, so far as men are concerned, two parties to the covenant. There are within the life of the Godhead two parties — God the Father and the Son, who is the mediator of the covenant, but so far as we who are the recipients of its blessings are concerned, we have no contribution to make at all.'[1]

The second case is where God makes a gracious covenant with men, as with Noah, Abraham and David. Again there are two parties, but now the parties are not equal. Let me again quote Dr Kevan: 'The New Testament word for covenant ... excludes the idea of two people or two parties — God and men — making an equal contribution, and reminds us that fundamentally this pledge which binds us to God and God to us is something in which God is laying down all the terms, and in which he also is meeting all the requirements.'[2] In the New Testament, then, a covenant is not a mutual agreement between God and man, but a sovereign act of God's free grace. The Lord initiates this covenant, and its purpose is always redemptive.

The old covenant

To appreciate the enormous significance of the new covenant we must first of all consider the old, or first, covenant. In New Testament Scripture this always refers to the law given through Moses at Mount Sinai. For example, we read in Hebrews:

> If there had been nothing wrong with that first covenant, no place would have been sought for another. But God found fault with the people and said:

> 'The time is coming,' declares the Lord,
>   'when I will make a new covenant
> with the house of Israel
>   and with the house of Judah.
> It will not be like the covenant
>   I made with their forefathers
> when I took them by the hand
>   to lead them out of Egypt,
> because they did not remain faithful to my
>   covenant,
>   and I turned away from them,' declares the Lord
>   (Heb. 8:7-9).

A few verses later, he continues, 'By calling this covenant "new", [God] has made the first one obsolete; and what is obsolete and ageing will soon disappear' (Heb. 8:13).

We shall return to this important passage presently, when we consider the nature of the new covenant. For the moment, however, we see that the old covenant refers to the law given on Sinai, when God brought his people out of Egypt. Hebrews makes it clear that this 'first' covenant was not a means by which the Israelites could be justified before God. Otherwise there would have been no need for a new one. Berkhof explains the purpose of the covenant of Sinai in these terms: 'The law [of Moses] served a twofold purpose in connection with the covenant of grace: (1) to increase the consciousness of sin (Rom. 3:20; 4:15; Gal. 3:19); and (2) to be a tutor unto Christ, Gal. 3:24).'[3]

Thus the old covenant could not save anyone. As Paul says, 'No one will be declared righteous in [God's] sight by observing the law; rather, through the law we become conscious of sin' (Rom. 3:20). The commandments are 'holy, righteous and good', but man cannot obey them because he is innately sinful (Rom. 7:12-14). We may try to keep them, of course. We may even succeed in an outward and partial way. Witness Paul's boast before his spiritual eyes were opened: 'As for legalistic righteousness, [I was] faultless' (Phil. 3:6). But in reality our law-keeping is always faulty. At best, it lacks the perfection and the consistency that God requires. At worst, the demands of the law actually excite us to sin, because there is rebellion in our hearts. All that the law can do, therefore, is to show us our sin and make us realize that we are indeed sinners, under the judgement of an altogether holy God. But in doing that it bids us flee to Christ for free salvation.

Of course, the law of Sinai also provided for human sin. The tabernacle was given as a meeting-place with God; sacrifices were offered for the cleansing of the people, and a priesthood was established to intercede for them. But even these provisions, being shadows of the true, or symbols of Christ, could not reconcile a sinner to his God, or cleanse his guilty conscience from its sin. They could only represent, and point forward to, the Lord Jesus Christ, 'the Lamb of God, who takes away the sin of the world' (John 1:29).

Thus the tabernacle pictures Christ, for he is our meeting-place with God. The priesthood also pictures Christ, for he is our great High Priest 'who always lives to intercede for [us]' (Heb. 7:25). And he is our sacrifice, for he gave himself for our sins.

The law, then, could only point; it could not save. So, as Hebrews confirms, there remained a need for a different covenant, a new provision under which the sinner *could* be reconciled to God. This new covenant is what Christ inaugurated when he died, 'the just for the unjust, that he might bring us to God' (1 Peter 3:18, NKJV).

The covenant of promise

But what about believers before the time of Christ? Was there no saving covenant for them? Clearly, there must have been, since many of them are held up to us in the New Testament as men of faith whose example we should follow (see e.g. Heb. 11). The answer to this dilemma is that they did have a saving covenant. It was called the covenant of promise (Gal. 3:15-18).

Although Hebrews calls the covenant of Sinai the 'first' covenant, it was not in fact the first in a chronological sense. Long before the law was given on Sinai, God had *anticipated* the new covenant in terms of promises made to various individuals, notably Noah, Abraham and David, who were all men of faith. Referring to this 'covenant of promise' as it was revealed to Abraham, Isaac and Jacob, Paul writes as follows: 'The law, introduced 430 years later [than Jacob], does not set aside the covenant previously established by God and thus do away with the promise. For if the inheritance depends on the law, then it no longer depends on a promise; but God in his grace gave it to Abraham through a promise' (Gal. 3:17-18). Notice that this covenant of promise, made with Abraham, was 'confirmed before by God in Christ' (NKJV). This shows that it was an anticipation of the new covenant, inaugurated by Jesus and commemorated at the Lord's Table.

As a further example of the covenant of promise, consider for a moment the covenant with Noah. Here we see all the basic ingredients of God's covenant mercy, and it is apparent that the covenant is not a partnership but rather God making and keeping his promises. We could, of course, illustrate the covenant of promise from the more familiar story of Abraham. But for a change, let us think about Noah.

In Genesis 3 we read how sin entered human experience. From then on sin becomes the dominant factor in human nature and in Genesis 4 we see the influence of sin spreading beyond Adam and Eve to their son Cain. Ultimately, in Genesis 5, we read of sin reigning throughout the human race. Mahalel lived 895 years and Methuselah 969 years, and so on. The list of patriarchs is long, but at the end of each personal history we read the recurring phrase, 'and then he died'. They died, as all men and women do, because they were sinners, and death is the wages of sin (Rom. 6:23). In death, therefore, we see the reign of sin at its most potent.

By the time we arrive at Genesis 6, sin's influence is total: 'The Lord saw how great man's wickedness on the earth had become, and that every inclination of the thoughts of his heart was only evil all the time.' God's verdict on sinful man was devastating: 'I will wipe mankind, whom I have created, from the face of the earth … for I am grieved that I have made them' (Gen. 6:5,7).

Noah lay under the wrath and judgement of God, along with the rest of mankind, for he too was a sinner. But this particular sinner was promised salvation, and it is in this that we begin to see the character of the covenant God. When, before time began, he foresaw man in sin and under the threat of judgement, God's heart prompted him to institute a plan of salvation, the covenant of redemption. According to this plan, he determined to redeem from their sin and lost condition 'a great multitude that no one could count' (Rev. 7:9). Those to be saved he 'chose … in [Christ] before the creation of the world, to be holy and blameless in his sight' (Eph. 1:4).

Let us be clear. These chosen ones were not selected for any good that God foresaw in them, but out of God's free, unmerited grace. In Genesis 6:8 we are told that 'Noah found favour in the eyes of the Lord' (NIV). A better translation is: 'Noah found grace...' (NKJV). Grace always speaks of the lack of merit on man's part and the abundance of mercy on God's. In effect, Noah did not find grace, but grace found Noah! The initiative, as always, was God's. The fact is that God chose Noah and not that Noah chose God. Noah did not earn grace because he was righteous and blameless (Gen. 6.9), for by definition grace cannot be earned.

James Montgomery Boice expresses it in the following words: 'Some people read these verses as if God chose Noah because he was righteous and lived a blameless life. But that is not the case and, in fact, to read it that way is to get it backward. Verse 9 does not come before verse 8, nor is there even a connecting or causal participle between them, as if to say, "Noah found grace because he was righteous." Actually, Noah's righteousness was the *product* of his having found favour and is therefore the proof of that favour, not its ground. This is a great biblical principle, namely, that the grace of God always comes before anything. We imagine, in our unsanctified state, that God loves us for what we are intrinsically or for what we have done, or can become. But God does not love us because of that, nor is he gracious to us because of that. He loves us solely because he loves us. He is gracious to us only because he is.'[4]

Into Noah's meritless situation came salvation which he did not, and could not, ever deserve, nor could he have achieved it by his own efforts. And the reason for this salvation is that God promised him, 'I will establish my covenant with you' (Gen. 6.18). Do you see the situation? On the one hand, God's holiness and hatred of sin set his judgement in action, and on the other, God's mercy and love put his eternal covenant to work. Both are in operation at the same time. Noah was not whisked away magically out of the ravages of the flood. He had to face that like all men. What the covenant did for Noah was to wrap him around with a God-given protection, namely the ark. This guaranteed him salvation when the waters of divine judgement came upon the earth. The ark was a picture of Christ, bearing the onslaught of the storm and thus protecting those who are 'in him' from judgement.

Genesis 6 ends with a fine testimony to Noah, that he 'did everything just as God commanded him'. This comes after God promised him the blessings of the covenant and as a consequence of that covenant. The covenant is not a covenant of works but a covenant of grace. Obedience is necessary, not to make the covenant work, and still less to bring the covenant about, but rather to enjoy its blessings. The only thing that keeps it working is the grace and mercy of God.

The new covenant

We saw earlier that the old Mosaic covenant was insufficient to provide salvation. This was not because the covenant was at fault, but because men are incapable of keeping God's laws. Hebrews 8:8, from which we have already quoted, says that God found fault 'with the people', not with the covenant. Nevertheless, if people were to be saved, a different covenant was required. And this is just what God *promised* to Abraham and others like him, and what he has *provided* in Christ.

We must now come to the verses which follow the passage in Hebrews 8 quoted earlier, since these describe God's new covenant in the following terms:

'This is the covenant I will make with the house of
    Israel
  after that time,' declares the Lord.
'I will put my laws in their minds
  and write them on their hearts.
I will be their God,
  and they will be my people.
No longer will a man teach his neighbour,
  or a man his brother, saying, "Know the Lord,"
because they will all know me,
  from the least of them to the greatest.
For I will forgive their wickedness
  and I will remember their sins no more'
                        (Heb. 8:10-12).

These words, of course, are a quotation from the Old
Testament (Jer. 31:31-34). Thus just as God made a
covenant of promise with Noah, Abraham and David, so
he inspired his prophets to look forward to the fulfilment
of the promise. That fulfilment is the new covenant in
Christ. The Old Testament believers named, along with
many others, were justified by faith in the coming Mes-
siah and his new covenant, even though they lived centuries before Christ came (see Rom. 4:2-8; Heb. 11).

The essential difference between the old and new
covenants, then, is that the new is written by God upon the
hearts and minds of men. It is not something external, but
internal; not a matter of religious observance, but of

spiritual reality. Leon Morris says, 'This means a radical break with the past. It represents a new approach to the problem of man's relationship to God. It is not that God's high standards are relaxed for one moment. God's law is to be put into their minds and written on their hearts. The moral law is being given a central place. The difference is that the law is now part of the people. It is within them, transforming them. They obey it because of what they are. This is more than the obeying of an external set of commands and ordinances. It points to a whole-hearted transformation. God's people will want to do God's will with mind and heart. Far from being a relaxation of moral demands or moral standards, these are heightened because they are now to be part of God's people's inmost being.'[5]

A better covenant

As well as being a new covenant, it is a superior one (Heb. 8:6), a better one (Heb. 7:22). In what sense is it better? There are many answers to this question. Jeremiah tells us, for example, that it is an everlasting covenant (Jer. 32:40). Isaiah shows us that the new covenant reaches far beyond the narrow confines of the Hebrew people, and declares that Christ would be a light for the Gentiles (Isa. 42:6). But above all, it is a better covenant because it is a covenant of *grace*.

Under the old covenant, the obedience of *men* to the law of God was essential if they were to receive its blessings, and this was its fatal weakness. Under the new covenant it is the obedience of *Christ* that secures for us the blessing of salvation. Christ, not Moses, is the mediator of this new covenant. The blessings come to us through him, and the strength and invincibility of the new covenant lie in the perfect life and obedience of Christ. During his life on earth, he satisfied the law of God in every particular, for he was 'without sin' (Heb. 4:15). And this perfect righteousness, earned as a man among men, is put to the account of all who trust in him for salvation. As Paul writes, 'God made him [Christ] who had no sin to be sin for us, so that in him we might become the righteousness of God' (2 Cor. 5:21).

But the covenant in Christ is better for another reason. It is a covenant made in his blood — that is, a covenant put into effect by his atoning death. The blood of bulls and goats cannot take away sin, but the precious blood of Christ is effective to this end: 'It was not with perishable things such as silver or gold that you were redeemed ... but with the precious blood of Christ, a lamb without blemish or defect' (1 Peter 1:18-19).

On the cross the new covenant, promised by God in Jeremiah 600 years previously, and even before that to Noah and Abraham, is ratified in the blood of the Lord Jesus Christ. The cup we take at the Lord's Supper is the symbol of both the blood of Christ and the covenant made in that blood. It is to us a sign of the grace of God and the guarantee of our salvation. The cross is now central in all God's dealings with man. It transforms everything. This is why Jesus said, 'This cup is the new covenant in my blood' (1 Cor. 11:25).

Notice that he did not say, 'the new covenant in my death'. To quote Dr Kevan again, 'The death of Christ and the blood of Christ are not strictly synonymous terms; because the blood of Christ indicates something more than the death of Christ. The blood of Christ gathers up into it all the connotation of sacrifice and of covenant and of guarantee.'[6] As with Abraham and Noah, God's grace finds us and establishes his covenant with us. He does not take us out of this world, but provides a sure protection from our guilt, judgement and sin. This protection is not a temporary place of safety, like the ark of wood, but a permanent 'hiding-place' from wrath and judgement, namely 'Christ and him crucified' (1 Cor. 2:2). It is Christ, then, who protects and sustains us against the ravages of sin and the storm of judgement:

His oath, his covenant and his blood,
Support me in the 'whelming flood;
When all around my soul gives way
He then is all my hope and stay.[7]

And eventually, when the threatened judgement comes,

Jesus, thy blood and righteousness
My beauty are, my glorious dress;
Midst flaming worlds, in these arrayed,
With joy shall I lift up my head.[8]

3.
'This is my body'

*'This is my body, which is for you... This cup is the
new covenant in my blood'* (1 Cor. 11:24,25).

The two words, 'This is...' have caused great controversy
in the church over the past two thousand years, but in the
early years of Christianity there was no such problem.
The early church leaders and theologians mostly taught
that the bread and the wine were symbolic and had a
spiritual meaning. This was also the teaching of Augus-
tine in the fourth century. It was not until 1215 that the
Roman Catholic Church officially propagated the doctrine of 'transubstantiation'. The word means 'a change
of substance' and is applied to the idea that the bread and
wine are literally changed into the body and blood of
Christ at the moment they are 'consecrated' by the priest
during the 'mass'.

Such teaching makes the mass much more than a
religious ceremony. The Roman Catholic *New York Cat-
echism* says, 'Jesus Christ gave us the sacrifice of the
Mass to leave to his church a visible sacrifice which

continues his sacrifice on the Cross until the end of time. The Mass is the same sacrifice as the sacrifice of the Cross. Holy Communion is the receiving of the body and blood of Jesus Christ under the appearance of bread and wine.' The Council of Trent said the same thing: 'The sacrifice in the Mass is identical with the sacrifice of the Cross, in as much as Jesus Christ is a priest and victim both. The only difference lies in the manner of offering, which is bloody upon the Cross and bloodless on our altars.'[1]

Once the priest has consecrated the bread (that is, the wafer) it is called 'the host', and when he lifts that host up he is, according to Roman Catholic teaching, actually offering to God the very body and blood of Christ as a sacrifice for the living and the dead. On what do they base these beliefs? It all stems from a fundamental misunderstanding of the words, 'This is...' It has led to what must be the greatest heresy ever concocted by man, namely that the sacrifice of Christ on the cross was not a once-and-for-all act but, to be effective, has to be repeated over and over again.

To deny that Christ's work upon the cross is a finished work is to deny the gospel, because it leaves the sinner with no certain hope of eternal salvation. The doctrine of the mass also, by implication, denies God's ability to provide a complete salvation for us in Christ, since it demands a continual daily sacrifice for sin. There can be no greater heresy than that. Loraine Boettner writes, 'The

Roman Catholic doctrine of the sacraments constitutes the most elaborate system of magic and ritual that any civilized religion ever invented, and from first to last it is designed to enhance the power and prestige of the clergy. In its fundamental ideas it is ... alien to the whole spirit of Christianity.'[2]

During the Reformation Luther and Calvin rejected the doctrine of the mass, but even they could not agree on the meaning of the words, 'This is my body.' Luther taught a doctrine called 'consubstantiation'. Of this, Berkhof writes, 'According to [Luther] bread and wine remain what they are, but there is in the Lord's Supper nevertheless a mysterious and miraculous real presence of the whole person of Christ, body and blood, in, under, and along with, the elements.'[3]

Calvin also taught that Christ is present in the communion service but that his presence is spiritual rather than physical. Boice explains that 'Calvin called this "the real presence" to indicate that a spiritual presence is every bit as real as a physical one.'[4]

The bread: what does 'This is...' really mean?

Jesus' words meant that the Passover bread was then, and should remain thereafter, a symbol and memorial of his body killed (and in that sense, broken) on the cross. He often used speech in a figurative or symbolic way. When the Saviour said, 'I am the door', it is clear that he did not want the statement to be understood literally but figuratively. John's Gospel is full of this kind of metaphor. It is interesting that when people insisted on interpreting what Jesus said literally instead of symbolically, the Scripture makes it clear that they were wrong. For instance, in Matthew 16:6, Jesus warns his disciples to be on their guard against 'the yeast of the Pharisees and Sadducees'. They interpreted this literally and said among themselves, 'It is because we didn't bring any bread' (v. 7). Jesus had to put them right, and we read, 'Then they understood that he was not telling them to guard against the yeast used in bread, but against the teaching of the Pharisees and Sadducees' (v. 12).

How do we know when Jesus is speaking literally and when he is speaking symbolically? The context of his words will tell us. The context of the Lord's Supper shows that the bread and wine have to be interpreted symbolically. As we have already seen, the context in question was that of the Passover meal. This was the annual remembrance by the Jewish people of their deliverance from slavery in Egypt by the intervention of Almighty God. That intervention culminated in the slaying of the Passover lamb, the breaking and eating of its body by the people and the sprinkling of its blood on the door-posts of their homes. God promised that when he saw the blood on the door-posts he would pass over that home and no judgement would touch those within.

That literally happened, but the New Testament makes it clear that it was also symbolic of a greater redemption that was to come. It was not accidental that Christ died at the time of Passover. The Jewish establishment desperately wanted to kill Jesus, but they would not have chosen to do so at the feast time, which was for them a special and holy ceremony. They did not want an execution to mar it, and they were also afraid of possible crowd reactions. But by his triumphant entry into Jerusalem at the beginning of Passover week, Jesus forced their hand. He chose to die at Passover because Passover illustrated the meaning of his death on the cross. It was a substitutionary death to purchase redemption for his people and to deliver them from the wrath and judgement of God.

That was the context of the first Lord's Supper. Jesus and his disciples, by consuming the lamb, bread and wine in the upper room, were symbolically re-enacting the redemption from Egypt hundreds of years before. But it did not stop at that. Jesus took the bread and wine and said, 'This is my body... This is my blood.' A moment's reflection shows that it would not make sense to take this literally, for at that moment Jesus' body was intact and his blood still coursed in his veins. He had to mean, 'This is symbolic of what I am going to do by my death on the cross.' The symbols, like those of the Passover feast itself, were intended to help us remember the act that purchased our redemption.

41

The blood

In the story of the Passover night in Egypt, the most important factor was the blood. Throughout the Old Testament, redemption was always by blood, and the whole sacrificial system was based upon this. 'It is the blood that makes atonement' (Lev. 17:11). Hebrews 9:22 reminds us, 'In fact, the law requires that nearly everything be cleansed with blood, and without the shedding of blood there is no forgiveness.' Why should this be? The answer is given in Leviticus 17:14: 'The life of every creature is its blood.' When blood is shed, the life of the victim is also sacrificed. As Isaiah tells us, speaking prophetically of Christ, 'He poured out his life unto death' (Isa. 53:12).

The same principle is maintained in the New Testament, only now it is no longer the blood of animals, but rather the blood of Christ that constitutes God's provision for the sinner's redemption. So in the New Testament the language of salvation continues to emphasize the pre-eminence of the blood. For example:

We are bought by the blood of God (Acts 20:28).

We are to have faith in Christ's blood (Rom. 3:25).

We are justified by Christ's blood (Rom. 5:9).

We have redemption through Christ's blood (Eph.1:7).

This continual use of the word 'blood' tells us something very important about the death of Jesus — it was a *sacrificial* death to make atonement for the sin of his people. The body was broken so that the blood could be shed. His infinitely valuable life was sacrificed and offered as a ransom for our souls. He said, 'The Son of man did not come to be served, but to serve, and to give his life as a ransom for many' (Mark 10:45).

The cup

Christ's use of the word 'cup' at the first Lord's Supper is also significant. Did he just mean the cup as a vessel to contain the wine, or was he alluding to the symbolic meaning of the word 'cup' in Scripture? He certainly used the word in this latter sense a few hours later in Gethsemane, when he prayed, 'My Father, if it is possible, may this cup be taken from me' (Matt. 26:39). It was the prospect of drinking the cup of God's wrath against sin that caused Jesus the crushing sorrow recorded in the previous verse: 'My soul is overwhelmed with sorrow to the point of death.' The sorrow was not caused by the prospect of death. Death was not the problem to Jesus that it is to us, for he knew it would restore him to the glory he had with the Father before creation. The problem for the Saviour was what was involved in his death, and that is what the word 'cup' refers to in his prayer in Gethsemane.

The idiom of 'drinking the cup' in the Old Testament refers predominantly to God's punishment of human sin. Isaiah cries,

Awake, awake!
   Rise up, O Jerusalem,
you who have drunk from the hand of the LORD
   the cup of his wrath,
you who have drained to its dregs
   the goblet that makes men stagger

(Isa. 51:17).

Likewise, Jeremiah records, 'This is what the LORD, the God of Israel, said to me: "Take from my hand this cup filled with the wine of my wrath and make all the nations to whom I send you drink it. When they drink it, they will stagger and go mad because of the sword I will send among them"' (Jer. 25:15-16).

Jesus had always known that one day this cup of God's wrath would be put into his hands. But now, on the eve of his crucifixion, he felt the terrible implications and consequences of it. He would be 'made sin' for us, as God laid our sin and guilt upon his Son. And in that process of atonement he would be separated from, and forsaken by, his Father (Ps. 22:1; Matt. 27:46). Jesus endured the consequences of sin to the utmost extent. So fully did he make himself one with sinful man that he entered into the dreadful state of being forsaken by God that is the lot of

44

unforgiven sinners. He died our death so that we might live to God.

If all this was in the mind of Christ when he spoke of 'the cup' in Gethsemane, it would be surprising if it was not also in his mind in the upper room, as he spoke of his blood that would be shed. The cup of the communion service should therefore remind us of the enormous cost to Christ of our salvation. But by the same token, it reminds us also of the riches of his grace and of the blessedness of those who trust in his atoning sacrifice. Paul writes, 'You know the grace of our Lord Jesus Christ, that though he was rich, yet for your sakes he became poor, so that you through his poverty might become rich' (2 Cor. 8:9).

> Death and the curse were in our cup;
> O Christ, 'twas full for thee!
> But thou hast drained the last dark drop,
> 'Tis empty now for me;
> That bitter cup, love drank it up,
> Now blessing's draught for me.[5]

4.
Remembrance

'Do this in remembrance of me' (1 Cor. 11:24).

What impresses us most as we read the account of the first Lord's Supper is the utter simplicity of it. There is no pomp or ceremony, no deeply veiled mystical element; we find just a group of men gathered around a simple table in an upper room. Its very simplicity is its glory. We should always be suspicious of a communion service that loses this basic simplicity. The elaborations that have been added to the original Lord's Supper by the church of Rome and others can only detract from its simple basic message and obscure a biblical understanding of the Lord's Supper.

Not a sacrifice

The principal purpose of the Lord's Supper is to remind Christians of Christ's death for sinners. It is not a sacrifice. In the previous chapter we saw how the Roman Catholic Church claims that 'Jesus Christ gave us the sacrifice of the Mass to leave to his church a visible sacrifice which continues his sacrifice on the Cross until the end of time. The Mass is the same sacrifice as the sacrifice of the Cross.' But this is totally misconceived. There are no sacrifices now in Christianity.

The last altar that God recognized was the cross and the last sacrifice was Christ, the Lamb of God. The New Testament makes this abundantly plain. Contrasting the new covenant with the old, Hebrews declares with devastating clarity: 'Day after day every priest stands and performs his religious duties; again and again he offers the same sacrifices, which can never take away sins. But when this priest [Christ] had offered for all time one sacrifice for sins, he sat down at the right hand of God ... because by one sacrifice he has made perfect for ever those who are being made holy' (Heb. 10:11-14). In the words of the Prayer Book, when we come to the table, the bread and wine remind us of this 'one full, perfect and sufficient sacrifice, oblation and offering for the sins of the world'. The symbols are a visible sermon, preaching 'Christ and him crucified'.

We do well to keep steadily in view the simplicity of the Lord's Supper. The less mystery and obscurity we attach to it, the better it will be for our souls. So we must firmly reject that unscriptural Roman Catholic notion that at the Lord's Table we are sacrificing Christ again. Equally, we must firmly reject what some Protestants seem to believe, that the mere formality of taking bread and wine does us some unspecified spiritual good. Those who come to the table with love in their hearts towards Christ will doubtless find that love strengthened and deepened. But the one who comes out of habit, with empty formality, will find no blessing. Empty he will come and empty he will go. Bishop Ryle said, 'The Lord's Supper was meant to increase and help the grace that a man has, but not to impart the grace that he has not. It was certainly never intended to make our peace with God, to justify, or to convert.'[1]

Remembering

'Do this', said Jesus, 'in remembrance of me.' But if we know nothing of peace with God, that peace that was made for sinners through his blood, shed on the cross (Col. 1:20), then we have nothing to remember. We cannot remember what we have never experienced. An example from ordinary life is that of Remembrance Day, the special day each November when Britain commemorates the end of the First World War in 1918. On that day we are meant to remember all those who gave their lives in both World Wars. But to most folk under the age of fifty there is actually no remembering on this day. They cannot remember the horrors of war, and the joy of its cessation, because they have never experienced it. They know no one who died in those wars. They may well respect and sympathize with what the day represents, but they cannot remember. But to those older people who fought in the war and saw friends die on the battlefield, or to those women who lost husbands and sons, the experience is burned indelibly upon their hearts and minds. Remembrance Day to them is not a meaningless ceremony. On that day they do more than feel respect and sympathy. They remember.

At the Lord's Table we are called upon by Jesus to remember something that happened 2,000 years ago. How can we do this in a meaningful way? How can we remember without its degenerating into a formal ceremony? There are many great historical events we remember that have lost all relevance to the original happenings. In Britain 'Guy Fawkes Day' on 5 November is one such example. Bonfires are lit and fireworks set off, and the children chant:

Remember, remember the fifth of November, Gunpowder, treason and plot.

But does anyone really remember that Guy Fawkes was involved in a Roman Catholic plot to blow up a Protestant parliament? Very few, if any, do; it is just an excuse to enjoy ourselves.

How can we prevent the Lord's Table from becoming merely a habit, an empty, meaningless ceremony? The answer is to realize that we are not called to remember just a historical event (though the death of Jesus was that), but something that has become (and remains) for us a personal experience. As a believer in Christ, I am remembering that 'The Son of God … loved me and gave himself for me' (Gal. 2:20). This is a reality that has profound meaning for us and should have a powerful influence upon our daily lives.

For you

'Take, eat', said Jesus. 'This is my body which is broken for you' (1 Cor. 11:24, NKJV). The words 'for you' obviously have a direct reference to the apostles in the upper room, but are not limited to them. When Jesus commanded this sacrament to be observed regularly until he comes again, he was clearly broadening its application to all believers in every generation. 'For you', therefore, includes us. The historical event of 2,000 years ago involves every single Christian personally. There is a sense in which all the great events in history, no matter when they occurred, affect us and influence the course of our lives. But the effect of history on our lives is consequential and indirect, whereas the death of Jesus involves believers directly and personally.

Jesus said that by his death he was doing something for us of which the bread and wine were reminders. When other people do things for you, there are two possible meanings. Either they are helping you do something you could do yourself, but by helping they save you time and effort; or they are doing something for you which you could not do yourself, and which, if it is not done for you, will not be done at all. The gospel makes it clear that when Christ died for us on the cross, he accomplished something that could never have been done in any other way. What Jesus did was unique. He died in our place as our substitute, and bore the wrath of God instead of us. By his death he made us free.

Our greatest problem is our sin and guilt. God takes this very seriously and the Bible teaches that our sin puts each of us under the curse of the law (Deut. 27:26). We are all guilty of sin, and therefore we are all under the curse. Without deliverance from this curse there can be no salvation, but only the fearful anticipation of judgement. Against this dark backcloth, Paul makes the incredible statement that 'Christ redeemed us from the curse of the law by becoming a curse for us' (Gal. 3:13). On the cross, Jesus took responsibility for our sin and guilt, and God laid on him all our violations of the holy law. He did it for his chosen ones, whom the Father gave to him before the foundation of the world, and all who put their trust in Christ alone for salvation thereby demonstrate their election of God. He became a curse *for us,* and faced the wrath and judgement of God *for us*. He did it so that we might be rescued from our rebellion and become 'dear children' of God. Jesus Christ, we are told, was 'born of a woman, born under law, to redeem those under law, that we might receive the full rights of sons' (Gal. 4:4-5).

This is the gospel, and when we come to the Lord's Table this is what we remember above all other things. As Christians we are to live our lives in the shadow of the cross. In other words, the declaration made at Calvary of the grace and mercy of God in Jesus Christ is to be remembered in such a way that it touches every facet of our lives. Therefore at the table it is not only a past event that must fill our thoughts, but also a present experience of the love of God to us in the Lord Jesus Christ. There can be no room for meaningless formality when our minds are taken up with the living Christ.

5.
Until he comes

'You proclaim the Lord's death until he comes'
(1 Cor. 11:26).

The message Paul received from the Lord is contained in
verses 23-25 of 1 Corinthians 11. These words are also
found in the accounts of the first Lord's Supper recorded
by Matthew, Mark and Luke. From verse 26 onwards, we
have Paul's teaching, rather than the words of Christ.
Nevertheless, this teaching was still 'received from the
Lord' in the sense that it was inspired by the Holy Spirit,
as is all Scripture. The apostle now shows us that, when
we come to the Lord's Table, we are to look forward to the
future as well as remembering the past. In doing so, the
church, and every believer individually, is proclaiming
the significance of what Christ has done for us on the
cross.

Proclamation

Paul writes, 'Whenever you eat this bread and drink this cup, you proclaim the Lord's death until he comes' (1 Cor. 11:26). Every time we eat the bread and drink the wine, therefore, we are in fact preaching the great truths of the gospel. We are proclaiming the fact of the Lord's death, its historical reality. We are proclaiming to our fellow-believers that our trust is in Christ alone. We are also proclaiming to an unseen audience, namely the powers of darkness, that Christ has made a public spectacle of them, triumphing over Satan, sin and death (Col. 2:15).

The death of Christ is no fairy story; it actually happened. Jesus was crucified under Pontius Pilate. I can remember being taught at theological college that Pilate never existed. It was argued that there was little, if any, evidence that this man was ever procurator of Judea and that this cast doubt on whether or not Christ was crucified. Then in 1961 a stone was found at Caesarea bearing the name of Pontius Pilate, and the Bible was vindicated yet again. But the believer does not need archaeology to validate the cross. Every time we come to the Lord's Supper we are reminding ourselves and the world that this was an event that really happened and one that changed the course of human history.

The Lord's Table also declares to the world that we are 'not ashamed of the gospel of Christ, for it is the power of

God to salvation for everyone who believes' (Rom. 1:16, NKJV). This simple act of remembrance is evidence that believers genuinely trust in Christ for their salvation; that they rely on Christ and him crucified for their acceptance with God, and not upon their own good works. It is tragic that this service is so distorted by some churches that it becomes the focal point of a religion of works. That is totally illogical, for no other act of worship declares more plainly the futility of human work and the sufficiency of that of Christ.

We also proclaim the effect that Christ's death has had on us personally. As we trust in Christ, our sins are forgiven and we have peace with God. The Lord's Supper is not an empty ceremony but a glorious declaration that because Christ died for us we are now new creatures in Christ, united to him by the power of divine love and the indwelling of his Holy Spirit. This 'personal proclamation' is addressed to ourselves and our fellow believers. As regards ourselves, it reminds us of a completed salvation and so strengthens our assurance. As addressed to fellow Christians, it encourages them in the faith.

However, in this chapter we want to explore the meaning of the words that Paul adds: 'until he comes'. We are to continue this wordless proclamation of the gospel until Christ returns in glory and power. We do not remember what Christ has done for us simply as an exercise in nostalgia, nor only as a testimony to the present benefits of the gospel; we are to celebrate the

Lord's Supper as a declaration that Christ will come again.

Thus the communion service embraces the whole glorious panorama of the Christian faith — past, present and future. According to the New Testament, the Second Coming of Christ will be a literal, physical and personal return of the Saviour to this world. The Second Coming of Christ is one of the most often repeated doctrines of Scripture, and twenty-three of the twenty-seven books that constitute the New Testament make reference to it. The Lord's Supper is a constant witness to this truth about Christ's return, and as such it is a service of confidence and hope.

Differences among believers on the Second Coming

It is impossible to observe the Lord's Supper properly unless we accept the truth of the Second Coming. How can we eat the bread and drink the cup 'until he comes' if we do not believe Jesus is coming again? But by believing in the Second Coming I do not mean believing a particular prophetic interpretation. Nothing has so divided believers as the various interpretations of the Second Coming. The controversy basically comes down to the meaning of the 'thousand years' (the 'millennium') referred to in Revelation 20, and on this subject there are three major views.

1. Postmillennialism teaches that the Second Coming of Christ will follow the millennium. The millennium, therefore, represents that part of human history leading up to the Lord's return.

2. Premillennialism maintains that Christ's second coming will precede the millennium. The millennium will therefore be a period when Christ reigns on the earth following his return.

3. Amillennialism, or non-millennialism, holds that the thousand years of Revelation 20 are not to be understood literally but figuratively, and that the millennium should not be viewed as an actual period of time.

The greatest Bible teachers have held different views on the Second Coming. For instance, Charles Hodge and Jonathan Edwards were postmillennialists; J. C. Ryle and Francis Schaeffer were premillennialists; and William Hendriksen and Martyn Lloyd-Jones held to amillennialism. The fact that such great men could differ on this doctrine should cause the rest of us to be cautious, and to avoid contentions with those fellow-believers who do not share our view. We may differ on interpretation, but all true Christians accept the certain fact that Christ will come again, because this is the plain teaching of Scripture. It is not my purpose in this book, therefore, to argue for one or other of these different opinions, but rather to emphasize that Christ's return is one of the things that he exhorts us to remember when we come to his table.

Confidence in his coming

To the natural mind the return of Christ in glory may seem an incredible thing to believe, but in reality it is no more incredible than Christ's first coming, which featured the incarnation and the virgin birth. In many ways the incarnation is the most amazing of all biblical truths. Once we accept the fact that 'The Word became flesh and made his dwelling among us' (John 1:14), then anything becomes possible. God did become man in the person of the Lord Jesus Christ; he did die in our place on the cross; he did rise from the dead; he did go back to heaven and he will return from heaven to this world. Of this we can be confident.

At Christ's ascension angels, who had proclaimed his first coming, declared, 'This same Jesus, who has been taken from you into heaven, will come back in the same way you have seen him go into heaven' (Acts 1:11). The Lord's Supper confirms all this and emphasizes that our belief in the Second Coming is not misplaced naïvety, but is based upon the word and promise of God.

In particular, our confidence is based on the fact that Jesus often spoke about his return, both in direct statement and in parables. As an example, let us turn to

Matthew 24-25, chapters that have been called 'the little apocalypse' because they teach so much about the last times and Christ's return. His disciples asked him, 'What will be the sign of your coming and of the end of the age?' (Matt. 24:3). Jesus warned them that false christs would come, deceiving many, but that he himself would not return until certain recognizable things had first occurred. Only after a period of tribulation would 'all the nations of the earth ... mourn' and 'see the Son of Man coming on the clouds of the sky with power and great glory' (Matt. 24:30).

Then Jesus proceeded to drive home the reality of his Second Coming with a series of parables such as the fig tree, the analogy with the days before the flood, the thief in the night and the evil servant who thought he could get away with anything because his master's coming was delayed (Matt. 24:32-51). Then he told what is perhaps the best-known of all the Second-Coming parables, the story of the wise and foolish virgins (Matt. 25:1-13). How relevant this is to our subject! Negatively, it warns us to beware the fate of the foolish virgins, who were without oil when the bridegroom came. The oil signifies the Holy Spirit, and the absence of oil denotes a nominal church that knows nothing of the ministry of that Spirit. What is this ministry? It is, said Jesus, to 'bring glory to me by taking from what is mine and making it known to you' (John 16:14). The wise virgins, by contrast, had oil in their lamps, and to spare, signifying a Spirit-filled, and thus Christ-centred, church prepared and waiting for its Lord's return. How can we 'keep ourselves awake' in this same expectation? The Lord's Table, with its constant reminder of his coming, is certainly one way by which the Lord helps us to be constantly prepared.

The Day of Judgement

Because the Lord's Table reminds us of Christ's coming again, it must also remind us of the final judgement. The concluding parable in 'the little apocalypse' relates to the judgement, when Christ will separate the believing 'sheep' from the professing but unbelieving 'goats' (Matt. 25:31-46). This tells us that Christ's coming will inaugurate the final reckoning, when the whole human race will stand before his throne of judgement. Thus the Lord's Table, by implication, also reminds us of that awesome and terrible event. In that day the blood of the new covenant will seem especially precious to those for whom Christ died. For it will cover them and hide them from God's wrath and righteous judgement against sin and those who practise it.

Christ's coming will be wonderful for some and dreadful for others. It will be great for Christians whose sins have been dealt with once for all and who now face no prospect of condemnation (Rom. 8:1). But for unbelievers it will be a dreadful and terrible day. Because of this the unbeliever tries desperately to convince himself that there will be no Second Coming, no judgement and no hell. Peter deals with such people when he says, 'In the last days scoffers will come, scoffing and following their own evil desires. They will say, "Where is this 'coming' he promised? Ever since our fathers died, everything goes on as it has since the beginning of creation"' (2 Peter 3:3-4).

If you have no Saviour, it is comforting to believe that there is no God to face. 'But,' says Peter, 'they deliberately forget that long ago by God's word the heavens existed and the earth was formed out of water and by water. By these waters also the world of that time was deluged and destroyed. By the same word the present heavens and earth are reserved for fire, being kept for the day of judgement and destruction of ungodly men' (2 Peter 3:5-7). The apostle tells us not to forget that 'With the Lord a day is like a thousand years, and a thousand years are like a day' (2 Peter 3:8). Any delay in the Second Coming is because of the grace and patience of God. He gives the unbeliever even more time to repent, but this situation will not go on for ever.

A glorious prospect

As terrible as this truth is for the unbeliever, the Second Coming brings a thrilling prospect to the Christian. In

Peter's words, 'We are looking forward to a new heaven and a new earth, the home of righteousness.' Such a prospect invites us at this present time to take courage and to seek holiness. 'So then,' continues the apostle, 'since you are looking forward to this, make every effort to be found spotless, blameless and at peace with him' (2 Peter 3:13,14).

The victory that Jesus won for us at the cross will have its glorious fulfilment at the Second Coming. What a prospect this is! One of the marks of a true believer is that he can delight in this prospect. The apostle Peter, preaching on the Day of Pentecost, quotes Joel's prophecy about the Second Coming:

> The sun will be turned to darkness
>> and the moon to blood
> before the coming of the great and dreadful day of
>> the LORD
>
> (Joel 2:31).

Clearly, this prophecy was fulfilled in part at Pentecost but, as Calvin points out, 'The prophet includes the whole kingdom of Christ, from the beginning to the end; and this is well understood, and in other places we have stated that the prophets commonly speak in this manner; for when the discourse is concerning Christ's kingdom, they sometimes refer to its commencement only, and sometimes they speak of its termination; but they often mark out by one delineation the whole course of the kingdom of Christ, from its beginning to its end; and such is the case here.'[1]

Calvin goes on to say, 'The prophet then means, that men persisting in their obstinacy shall meet with something more grievous and more ruinous than the evils of this life, for they must all at last stand before the tribunal of the celestial Judge; for the day of Jehovah, great and terrible, will come. He refers, in this sentence, to unbelievers and rebels against God; for when Christ shall come, he will be a redeemer to the godly; no day in their whole life will shine on them so pleasantly; so far will this day be from bringing terror and fear to them, that they are bidden, while expecting it, to lift up their heads, which is a token of cheerfulness and joy.'[2]

Comfort

The prospect of the Lord's return is a great comfort to Christians. It is something to cherish amidst the difficulties, adversities and frustrations of the present day. So when we come to the Lord's Supper, and are reminded of all that we have in Christ and that he will come again, these comforts should flood into our hearts and minds. Our present sufferings are very real, but they are 'not worth comparing with the glory that will be revealed in us' (Rom. 8:18). The glory anticipated by the Christian has nothing to do with the praise of men. It means, rather, to be for ever with the Lord, free from the effects and burden of sin; free to serve and worship him in glory; free to enjoy all that Christ died to obtain for us; free to be his spotless, glorious bride, beloved of God before time began. It is the ultimate end of our salvation. He is coming to take us home, to be with him in heaven for ever. How pleasant a prospect! How complete its comfort! Let the apostle John tell us in the words of inspired Scripture, as he describes the eternal city of God and of the Lamb: 'I did not see a temple in the city, because the Lord God Almighty and the Lamb are its temple. The city does not need the sun or the moon to shine on it, for the glory of God gives it light, and the Lamb is its lamp. The nations will walk by its light, and the kings of the earth will bring their splendour into it' (Rev. 21:22-24).

When Christ returns there will be no more Lord's Suppers. There will be no need to remember, because we shall be with him for ever. There will be no need to look forward, because he will be with us and we shall see him and be like him. And we shall go on for all eternity proclaiming the praises of the Lamb upon his throne.

6.
An unworthy manner

'Therefore, whoever eats the bread or drinks the cup of the Lord in an unworthy manner will be guilty of sinning against the body and blood of the Lord'
(1 Cor. 11:27).

The Lord's Supper commemorates the atoning death of Jesus on behalf of his people. The cross was God's one and only answer to our sin. So when we take the bread and wine we are saying, loud and clear, that we are sinners, condemned in the sight of the holy God. We are acknowledging that we are guilty men and women who deserve nothing but punishment and hell. But we are also saying that though we deserve hell, God in grace and love has dealt with our sins and we are saved. We are testifying that our hope is in Christ alone and we delight in his shed blood, by which we have been made acceptable to God. The Lord's Supper is only for those who can say these things.

For an unsaved person to take the bread and wine, therefore, is certainly to eat and drink in an unworthy manner, and we shall consider this more fully in chapter

8. However, the context of 1 Corinthians 11 shows that Paul is not talking here about the unsaved, but about born-again believers who eat and drink unworthily. This is clear from verse 32, where he contrasts them with the world, and verse 33, where he calls them 'my brothers'. What does it mean, then, to partake of the Lord's Supper in an unworthy manner?

Love feasts

The church at Corinth was a strange church. It abounded in spiritual gifts yet lacked the greatest gift of all, which is love, as Paul demonstrates clearly in 1 Corinthians 13. Since God himself is love (1 John 4:8), there is no substitute for love in the church. This implies that at Corinth nearly everything the church did was polluted. The church was spiritually immature; the gifts of the Holy Spirit were misused; there were divisions over the preaching; immorality was accepted and indulged; and their observation of the Lord's Supper was a disgrace.

Before the actual sacrament they held what they called a 'love feast', as we have seen. To these social gatherings everyone brought their own food. Some had plenty whilst others had very little (1 Cor. 11:21). The whole thing degenerated into selfishness and one-upmanship. There was no sharing, no concern for those in poor circumstances. All of this Paul fiercely condemns in verse 22.

What the apostle is saying here is that the behaviour of some of the Corinthian believers at the love feasts meant that they were coming to the Lord's Supper in an unworthy manner. They were behaving like the unregenerate and not as the redeemed of the Lord should.

But the worst thing was that these so-called 'love feasts' merged into the Lord's Supper, so that their reprehensible behaviour at the former spilled over into the latter. Charles Hodge puts it like this: 'The way in which the Corinthians ate unworthily was that they treated the Lord's Table as though it were their own; making no distinction between the Lord's Supper and an ordinary meal; coming together to satisfy their hunger, and not to feed on the body and blood of Christ; and refusing to commune with their poorer brethren. This, though one, is not the only way in which men may eat and drink unworthily. All that is necessary to observe is, that the warning is directly against the careless and profane, and not against the timid and the doubting.'[1]

No sense of sin

We eat and drink unworthily if we do not come with a sense of sin. It is to come without a clear recognition of personal unworthiness. As Hodge says, the warning is not aimed at those who feel unworthy, or who doubt their own qualifications to attend. Quite the reverse is true! It is only those who recognize their great need, and have a full view of their unworthiness, who properly take the Lord's Supper.

To come unworthily, then, is to come in a careless, irreverent spirit; it is to demonstrate, either by words or actions, that we have not understood the meaning of the Saviour's death. It is equivalent to behaving like those who crucified Christ, who had no perception or appreciation of the meaning of the cross. It is to be 'guilty of sinning against the body and blood of the Lord' — that is, guilty of profaning and despising the atoning sacrifice of Christ. This is a very serious sin, and Paul warns that if we do not do something about it, God will. He will bring judgement upon the church, not in the sense of eternal judgement (we are delivered from that), but the temporal judgement described in 1 Corinthians 11:29-32.

Judgement on the church's sin

What corrective action does God takes in such a situation? Paul explains: 'Anyone who eats and drinks without recognizing the body of the Lord eats and drinks judgement on himself. That is why many among you are weak and sick, and a number of you have fallen asleep' (1 Cor. 11:29-30).

'Falling asleep' here is a reference to death. The apostle is telling the Corinthians that God had sent physical afflictions, ill health and even death among them because they were sinning in this manner. There is a tendency today to think that God only operates in the spiritual realm, and that he does not interfere with people in their normal lives. But Scripture teaches the very opposite — namely that God is constantly active in providence. Far from this constituting 'interference', it is the sovereign activity of one who 'works out everything in conformity with the purpose of his will' (Eph. 1:11). Christians rejoice in the knowledge that 'In all things God works for the good of those who love him' (Rom. 8:28), but this implies the same sovereign involvement in human affairs as does the judgement of which Paul speaks in this passage. We cannot accept that God blesses us through providence, and then deny his right and ability to chastise his erring children in the same way.

We must be careful not to think that illness and death are necessarily, or even normally, attributable to the sin of the individuals concerned. The Scripture makes this matter quite plain. For example, in John 9:1-4, the disciples wanted to blame someone's sin for a man's blindness. But Jesus answered, 'Neither this man nor his parents sinned ... but this happened so that the work of God might be displayed in his life.' We cannot make a necessary connection between suffering and sin, but such a connection does sometimes exist. This was the case at Corinth. Sickness and premature death were afflicting the members of that church as a direct result of their behaviour at the Lord's Table and the attitudes that lay behind it. God was judging his people, and he can and will do so today if similar problems emerge.

We may err like the Corinthians without doing so in exactly the same way. These days, churches seldom hold love feasts before the Lord's Table, so the specific problems of gluttony and indifference to others that bedevilled the Corinthian church do not normally arise. But the same perverse spirit may be present in a church as that which had infected the Corinthians. Party spirit, backbiting and criticism, fleshly indulgence, spiritual laziness and immaturity, self-importance, misuse of gifts, lack of love — these and many other things may bring God's judgement upon us if we do not watch and pray.

Notice finally, however, that the purpose of this kind of judgement is to restore the church to fellowship with God and to protect its members from eternal judgement. Paul writes, 'When we are judged by the Lord, we are being disciplined so that we will not be condemned with the world' (1 Cor. 11:32). Although the same word is used in both instances, we must therefore, distinguish God's judgements on the church, which are really chastisements, or the exercise of discipline, from his judgement on the world. The purpose of discipline is to restore and bless, as Hebrews testifies: 'No discipline seems pleasant at the time, but painful. Later on, however, it produces a harvest of righteousness and peace for those who have been trained by it' (Heb. 12:11).

We need to examine ourselves, as we shall see in the next section.

How should a Christian come to the Lord's Supper?

Examine yourselves

Therefore, urges the apostle, 'A man ought to examine himself before he eats of the bread and drinks of the cup' (1 Cor. 11:28). When Paul urges us to examine ourselves he is not referring to a morbid introspection that robs us of our joy and assurance. He means that we are to be sure that we are at peace with God and with our fellow-believers.

Peace with God comes to us as a result of the justifying grace of God and was purchased for us at the cross. The table reminds us of this. We are sinners saved by grace. But the grace which saves us also 'teaches us to say "No" to ungodliness and worldly passions, and to live self-controlled, upright and godly lives in this present age' (Titus 2:12). Peace with God includes walking with the Lord and living in a state of perpetual fellowship with him. As John tells us, 'If we walk in the light, as he is in the light, we have fellowship with one another, and the blood of Jesus, his Son, purifies us from all sin' (1 John 1:7).

This Scripture reminds us that fellowship with God does not require sinlessness, for if it did, none of us could come. But it does mean that we come to the table in the spirit of what the death of Christ signifies. Paul expresses that spirit in ringing words: 'Do you not know that your body is a temple of the Holy Spirit...? You are not your own; you were bought at a price. Therefore honour God with your body' (1 Cor. 6:20). We are no longer our own; we have been bought with a price; and we must live to please Christ, not ourselves. We may fail in this — too often for comfort — but it is what we desire and, with the Holy Spirit's help, what we seek to achieve. Self-examination means caring about God and about our own Christian lives. Anything less will lead us to eat and drink in an unworthy manner. The old saints used to talk about 'keeping short accounts with God'. By this they meant that all known sin should be confessed and repented of daily.

To be at peace with our fellow-Christians is in some ways a more difficult thing. This is because peace with God depends exclusively upon the righteousness of Christ, and its imputation to us. When that peace is marred by our sin, we have only to confess and repent of that sin, and God graciously forgives us for the sake of Christ. Peace with one another, on the other hand, depends on our mortifying our sin and walking in the Spirit (Rom. 8:13; Gal. 5:16). Clearly, at Corinth this was a significant problem, and more often than not it is the problem of our churches today. It takes many forms.

For example, it is not unknown for a deacon to avoid being the one who serves the bread and wine to a fellow-believer with whom he is out of fellowship. Or perhaps we acknowledge that it is a sin for us to be at the same Lord's Table with someone against whom we entertain bitter thoughts, and yet we take comfort in the idea that Christ's blood forgives all sin, and go on in our bitterness. If that is what we think, we had better read 1 Corinthians 11:27-33 again, very slowly. Maybe you piously refuse to sit at the table with someone who has offended you, and call that honesty. So your sin of separation from a brother is perpetuated, and you add to it the sin of disobeying the Lord's command to remember his death in the sacrament.

It may seem easier not to deal with the problem but to avoid it. But the regular celebration of the Lord's Supper denies us this way out, and forces us to face up to the difficulty. It should remind us that there is no place in the Christian life for tensions and squabbles between believers. The sacrifice we are remembering tells us that we are all sinners, all guilty, and all totally unworthy. What right have we, then, to be annoyed, or angry, or bitter, with a fellow-believer? Such an attitude denies the very meaning of the Lord's Table, since it is based on the erroneous claim that 'I have been wronged and I am in the right.' The message of the blood of Christ is that none of us is right before a holy God. And if God, for Christ's sake, has forgiven us, then we must forgive others. We cannot deny

73

forgiveness to others while at the same time expecting to receive it from the Lord.

We are prone to consign fellow-believers to the scrap heap if they upset or offend us, and write them off as of no further use. But remember that those we write off in this way, God loves and Christ has redeemed. Those we will not speak to, God still speaks to.

Dealing with the problem

So how do we deal with damaged or shattered relationships among believers? What does God expect us to do about strained relationships in the church? The Lord himself provides the answer: 'Therefore, if you are offering your gift at the altar and there remember that your brother has something against you, leave your gift there in front of the altar. First go and be reconciled to your brother; then come and offer your gift' (Matt. 5:23-24). 'If your brother sins against you, go and show him his fault, just between the two of you. If he listens to you, you have won your brother over. But if he will not listen, take one or two others along, so that every matter may be established by the testimony of two or three witnesses. If he refuses to listen to them, tell it to the church; and if he refuses to listen even to the church, treat him as you would a pagan or a tax collector' (Matt. 18:15-17).

Both these passages put the responsibility upon us to take the initiative in putting matters right. Matthew 18 is particularly clear on the order of events to be followed. If you follow this order there may come a time when you can do no more. But you will have tried; you will have followed the instructions of your Lord. The situation will grieve you but there will be no bitterness in your heart, only sadness. Spurgeon said, 'From the first personal visit of the injured brother down to the last act of disownment, nothing has been done vindictively, but all has been affectionately carried out, with the view of setting the brother right. The trespasser who will not be reconciled has incurred much guilt by resisting the attempts of love, made in obedience to the command of the great Head of the church.'[2]

If we take seriously the communion or fellowship aspect of the Lord's Supper, such sad occurrences will be rare in the life of the church. The Lord's Table gives us a splendid and regular opportunity of searching our hearts, examining our consciences and putting right those things which are wrong between us and our brethren, long before these problems escalate into crises.

7.
Communion

'The cup of blessing which we bless, is it not the communion of the blood of Christ? The bread which we break, is it not the communion of the body of Christ?'
(1 Cor. 10:16, AV).

To many Christians the most popular way of referring to the Lord's Supper is to call it the communion service. The phrase originates from the Authorized Version rendering of 1 Corinthians 10:16. The Greek word is *'koinonia'* which is translated 'participation' in the NIV, and very often in both versions is translated 'fellowship'. For instance, in Acts 2:42 and 1 Corinthians 1:9 both the AV and the NIV translate the Greek *'koinonia'* as 'fellowship'.

Fellowship

Fellowship with other believers is central to authentic Christian experience. A. W. Tozer writes, 'The word "fellowship", in spite of its abuses, is still a beautiful and meaningful word. When rightly understood it means the same as the word "communion", that is, the act and condition of sharing together in some common blessing by numbers of persons. The communion of saints, then, means an intimate and loving sharing together of certain spiritual blessings by persons who are on an equal footing before the blessing in which they share.'[1] The apostle Paul had cause to thank God every time he remembered the Philippians, for their 'fellowship in the gospel' (NKJV), and because they were partakers with him of God's grace (Phil. 1:3,5,7). We should feel the same about our fellow believers.

The communion service is a fellowship service and, according to Paul, this fellowship is brought about by the Holy Spirit. He writes, 'May the grace of the Lord Jesus Christ, and the love of God, and the fellowship of the Holy Spirit be with you all' (2 Cor. 13:14). The Holy Spirit brings about the new birth and convicts us of sin and in doing so brings us in repentance and faith to Christ. In this way, the Spirit brings us into fellowship with God. This is what salvation is all about, but it does not end there. God's purpose is not that millions of isolated individuals should love him on their own, but that the church, the whole body of Christ, should adore and worship him together.

Thus one of the main activities of the Holy Spirit is to bring Christians into fellowship with each other. The church is 'a dwelling in which God lives by his Spirit'

(Eph. 2:22), and its fellowship is that *of* the Holy Spirit. Paul stresses this in 1 Corinthians 12:13: 'For we were all baptized by one Spirit into one body — whether Jews or Greeks, slave or free — and we were all given the one Spirit to drink.' It does not matter what our background was before we became Christians; Jew and Gentile, slave and free were the extremes of the first century, and Paul is telling us that even such extremes are blended by the Spirit into the church of Christ. When, by salvation, we are brought into fellowship with Christ, we are also brought into fellowship with one another. Fellowship is participation with others in Christ.

The church is a people called out of the world but also called to be together, and the word 'communion' stands for the togetherness of Christian experience. So when we refer to the Lord's Supper as the communion service we refer not only to fellowship with God, but also to fellowship between believers. This being so, we have to conclude that the sacrament tells us a great deal about the New Testament concept of the church.

The church together

We must observe the Lord's Supper together because we cannot properly observe it on our own. There are many things we can do on our own: we can pray, sing, worship, read our Bibles, and so on. But we cannot biblically observe the Lord's Supper on our own. It is a fellowship service and you cannot have fellowship with yourself. In Acts 20:7 Luke is describing an activity of the church: 'On the first day of the week we came together to break bread.' This is a statement of fact, but it is also a statement of necessity. In order to 'break bread' they needed to 'come together'. And in the great passage on the communion service in 1 Corinthians 11 the phrase 'come together' occurs four times (verses 18,20,33,34). The communion service belongs to the church, the company of believers, only as they come together.

We have seen that in the Lord's Supper we do a number of things. We 'remember', we 'proclaim', we 'look forward' — all these activities are centred on Christ and we do them because we love him. But, says the Bible, our love of Christ unites us with others who love him too. That is, if we love Jesus, we will also love his people. The communion service is an expression of this love. It tells us that we need one another and we cannot get along without one another. Sometimes you hear a Christian say about another believer, 'I can't get on with him.' The Lord's Supper tells us we cannot get on without him!

Fellowship with one another is evidence of our fellowship with Christ, and the New Testament will not allow us to evade this conclusion. 'If anyone says, "I love God," yet hates his brother, he is a liar. For anyone who does not love his brother, whom he has seen, cannot love God, whom he has not seen. And he has given us this command: Whoever loves God must also love his brother' (1 John 4:20-21).

It is significant that the main New Testament teaching on the Lord's Supper is found in this particular epistle. Ernest Kevan writes, 'The first letter to the Corinthians was written to them to check their excessive individualism. One of the results of the quickening grace of the Holy Spirit in the heart of a sinner is not only to bring him to God, but to heighten all his powers. This occasionally creates an excess of individualism in the believer... This might possibly account for the divisions and difficulties that appeared in the church at Corinth and which sometimes appear in our own.'[2] An extreme individualism, in which everyone does his own thing and stresses his own ideas, is a denial of the fellowship of the Holy Spirit. The Lord's Table, as a communion service, emphasizes that 'We, who are many, are one body; for we all partake of the one bread' (1 Cor. 10:17). Let us treasure and cultivate our oneness in Christ, for by doing so we reveal and honour Christ himself.

Physically and spiritually

When we celebrate the Lord's Supper we are to be physically together. To separate yourself from other

Christians for no good reason is sinful. Old age or illness or family responsibilities may make it impossible at times for us to join with other believers, but nothing else should prevent us doing so. We are not to 'give up meeting together' (Heb. 10:25). And it is no use saying piously, 'I was with you in spirit, if not in body.' That is not good enough. In certain circumstances it may be understandable, but it is not what God wants from us. The true fellowship of the Holy Spirit requires a joint act of many believers at one time in one place — that is communion.

But mere physical proximity is not enough. We should also be together spiritually. It is true that there have always been differences among Christians. From New Testament times onward this has been the case, but differences should not inevitably lead to divisions and quarrels. The Lord's Supper brings us together as sinners saved by grace. That is the basis of our communion and it is the only source of our fellowship. If fellowship were dependent upon our all having exactly the same beliefs and emphases, then it would only be a matter of time before you could hold your communion service in a telephone box!

This does not mean, of course, that doctrinal stands and strongly held beliefs are wrong. To maintain that viewpoint you would have to reject large portions of the New Testament. But it does mean that we should be able to differ from one another without breaking fellowship. When we gather around the Lord's Table it is not on the basis of our theological views, or the gifts of the Spirit, but on the fact that we are all sinners and we have come in repentance and faith to Jesus, who alone can save us.

Of course, we must be in agreement on the fundamentals of the gospel. No church could exist for very long if its members held widely different beliefs on key doctrines. But one of the privileges of being part of a church is to be exposed to other believers who may not see things exactly as we do, but none the less love the Lord Jesus Christ in sincerity and truth. Speaking of certain people in the fellowship of the church, J. C. Ryle says, 'Such a man's repentance may be very imperfect. Never mind! Is it real? Does he truly repent at all? — His faith in Christ may be very weak. Never mind! Is it real? A penny is as truly the current coin of the realm, and as fully stamped with the Queen's image as a sovereign. His charity may be very defective in quantity and degree. Never mind! Is it genuine? The grand test of a man's Christianity is not the quantity of grace he has got, but whether he has any grace at all. The first twelve communicants, when Christ himself gave the bread and wine, were weak indeed — weak in knowledge, weak in faith, weak in courage, weak in patience, weak in love! But eleven of them had that about them which outweighed all defects; they were real, genuine, sincere and true.'[3]

Let us then enjoy 'the communion of saints', knowing that our sainthood is none of our doing, but consists in the imputed righteousness of Christ, which is 'through faith in Jesus Christ to all who believe' (Rom. 3:22).

8.
Who should come to the Lord's Supper?

'We, who are many, are one body, for we all partake of the one loaf' (1 Cor. 10:17).

The Lord's Table is for the Lord's people, and no one else. In many churches, sadly, there is no perception of this basic truth, and all and sundry are welcomed to the 'communion service', whatever their spiritual condition, or even whether or not they have made a profession of faith. Some consider that this is the correct approach, believing that the Lord's Supper is an evangelistic tool or a 'converting ordinance'. But to urge unsaved people to attend is not to do them good, but harm. The Lord's Supper is not a converting or justifying ordinance. As J. C. Ryle says, 'If a man goes to the table unconverted or unforgiven, he will come away no better at all.'[1]

The plain truth is that the Lord's Supper was not meant for dead souls, but for living ones. To quote Ryle again, 'The careless, the ignorant and the wilfully wicked, so long as they continue in that state, are no more fit to come to the communion rail than a corpse is fit to sit down at a king's feast. To enjoy a spiritual feast we must have a spiritual heart, and taste, and appetite. To suppose that Christ's ordinances can do good to an unspiritual man, is as foolish as to put bread and wine into the mouth of a dead person.'[2]

On the contrary, for an unbeliever to be denied access to the Lord's Table may be the means of his conversion. Howel Harris, the great Welsh preacher of the eighteenth century, before he was saved was brought to think seriously about his spiritual condition when he heard his parish minister say, 'If you are not fit to come to the Lord's Table, you are not fit to live, nor fit to die.' No person should rest content to be unqualified to come to the table.

The saved should come

If you are saved, however, you should come and let nothing stop you. How frequently we receive the Lord's Supper will depend upon the tradition of the church we attend. Some churches observe the sacrament every week, others less frequently; and it is for each church to determine for itself. The Lord said, 'Do this, whenever you drink it...', and Paul adds, 'Whenever you eat this bread and drink this cup...' (1 Cor. 11:25,26). The word 'whenever' (or 'as often', AV) would seem to indicate that there was no fixed interval between celebrations. At one extreme, a daily observance may be indicated by some Scriptures such as Acts 2:46, while at the other extreme the analogy with the Passover would suggest an annual celebration. There are churches which practise both of these extremes, and who is to say one is right and the other wrong? What is certain is that we have a command from the Lord that it should be done regularly. And when your church meets around the Lord's Table, if at all possible, you should be there.

Protecting the table of the Lord

From everything we have seen, then, it should be obvious that only believers ought to take the bread and wine of the Lord's Supper. Most Christians and churches probably agree with this, but how can it be enforced? How do we prevent unbelievers from attending? The church has grappled with this problem for centuries and different groups of churches have come up with different answers. Some insist that only signed-up church members can attend, and these are easily distinguished from outsiders. Others allow only those baptized by immersion to attend, or only those who have been 'confirmed'. Yet others require non-members who wish to attend to sign a declaration of faith before they can be admitted to the service.

The list of solutions to the problem is long, but each of

them also succeeds in keeping some believers from the table. Thus Spurgeon would be excluded from a 'confirmed-persons-only' table, while Ryle would be banned from a Baptist table. It has not been unknown for a paedo-baptist to preach acceptably in a Baptist church and then be asked to leave before the communion service. Although he could preach to them, he could not break bread with them. That cannot be right. Indeed such 'solutions' cause as many problems as they solve.

Another remedy adopted by some churches is to move the sacrament from the Sunday services and hold it during the mid-week service in the knowledge that few, if any, unbelievers will attend a prayer meeting. Other Christians have despaired of ever finding a satisfactory answer and they say, 'It is the Lord's Table, not ours, and we have no right to prevent anyone from attending.' They simply invite those who love the Lord to come, and thus put the responsibility upon the recipient. In support of this approach it is sometimes argued that Jesus did not prevent Judas attending the first communion service, and that should be our example.

Why bother to protect the table?

Why should we bother with this matter? Is it really important? Of course there are bigger problems facing the church than this, but it is not unimportant.

If unbelievers partake of the Lord's Supper with believers they may be physically together but cannot be spiritually together. There can be no communion with Christians if there is not union with Christ. If believers and unbelievers sit at the same Lord's Table it removes any real meaning from the word 'communion'. Fellowship is much more than friendship. It is possible to have a friendship with an unbeliever and to enjoy each other's company, but that is not fellowship. True fellowship is based on a common experience of the grace of God in Christ. It is crucial for fellowship that both parties should be 'in Christ'.

The problem is at its worst when the unbelievers in question think they are believers. They may deny the deity of Christ, the resurrection, or the necessity of the new birth; they may on the other hand accept the teaching of the church but have no personal experience of salvation; but they may still consider themselves to be Christians. Moreover, if a church is slack on its standards for church membership this situation becomes almost inevitable. The problem is not then one of the purity of the Lord's Table, but the more basic one of what is a Christian church?

At the Lord's Supper we are remembering Christ, proclaiming his death and looking forward to his return. If we take seriously what we are doing, then we should make every effort to see that all who partake can genuinely do these things. It is no kindness to a man to let him think he is acceptable to God when everything about his beliefs and behaviour denies that this is so.

Judas

Whether or not Judas was actually present when Jesus instituted the Lord's Supper has been a matter of controversy for centuries. Calvin and Ryle said he was, whereas Jonathan Edwards, John Brown and William Hendriksen said he was not. I believe that John Brown was right when he wrote, 'It seems plainly to have been our Lord's purpose to get rid of the presence of the traitor before giving a pledge of his love, in the ordinance of the Supper, to his true-hearted disciples.'[3]

It is important to remember that two events were interwoven in the upper room — the celebration of the Passover and the inauguration of the Lord's Supper. For instance, the bread dipped into the dish in John 13:26-30 is not the bread of the Lord's Supper, but the Passover bread dipped into the paschal dish. John's Gospel does not mention the bread and wine of the communion at all. Matthew 26:23 and Mark 14:20 tell us that the dipping of the bread took place before the Lord's Supper, and John 13:30 says that Judas left the room as soon as the Passover bread was given to him. This order of events seems to make it clear that Judas was not at the Lord's Supper, yet

Luke 22:21 has the betrayer still present when the bread and wine of the Lord's Supper are distributed.

How are we to deal with this problem? The Gospel writers were not reporters recording every detail in precise order. As John tells us, they were selective (John 21:25). Furthermore, the sequence of recorded events is not always chronological. Leon Morris says, 'If Luke is writing in chronological order, then Judas was one of those who shared in the first service of holy communion. Doubt is raised because Matthew and Mark have this prophecy of the betrayal (after which Judas presumably left speedily) before that communion. However, none of these evangelists specifically places these events in sequence and we must remain uncertain.'[4] Nevertheless, if we are asking whether or not Judas was at the first Lord's Supper, the evidence of three of the four Gospel writers is that he was not. On this view, it is Luke who departs from chronological order, describing first the institution of the Lord's Supper as the subject of most significance to him, and then appending the prediction of betrayal.

Commenting on the words, 'What you are about to do, do quickly' (John 13:27), John Brown writes, 'It was also a clear intimation to Judas that he [Jesus] wished him to withdraw. He had given him many hints since he had first said, "Ye are clean, but not all," but the brazen-faced traitor had disregarded them all. He now, in terms courteous indeed, but too plain to be misunderstood, bids him

89

withdraw. He could no longer endure his presence; he wished to open his heart to his faithful followers, and to say to them much to which it was unmeet that such ears as Judas's should listen. He therefore, in these words, gives him, as it were, a final discharge from his service.'[5] If Brown is correct in this statement and the one quoted earlier then Jesus quite deliberately dismissed Judas from the room before the Lord's Supper took place.

This, then, sets the pattern for us. As far as is humanly possible, we should allow only believers to break bread at our communion services. This can be done, firstly, by making it very clear in the announcement, and in the introduction to the service, that the Lord's Table is only for those trusting in Christ alone for salvation. Only such should partake of the elements. Secondly, if known unbelievers do seek to attend, they should be taken on one side and the matter explained to them courteously. In suitable cases, an offer can be made to discuss the matter at leisure, since this could create an opening for the gospel with that particular person. There is no easy answer to this matter, but there are things like this that we can do.

A lesson from church history

The famous New England minister Jonathan Edwards had great difficulties with this matter in his church at Northampton, in the eighteenth century. The previous pastor, Edwards' grandfather Dr Stoddard, believed 'that unconverted persons, considered as such, had a right in the sight of God, or by his appointment, to the sacrament of the Lord's Supper'.[6]

Edwards disagreed: 'The actions of the communicants at the Lord's Table have as expressive and significant a language, as the most solemn words. When a person in this ordinance takes and eats and drinks those things which represent Christ, the plain meaning and implicit profession of these his actions, is this: I take this crucified Jesus as my Saviour, my sweetest food, my chief portion, and the life of my soul, consenting to acquiesce in him as such, and to hunger and thirst after him only, renouncing all other saviours, and all other portions, for his sake. The actions, thus interpreted, are a proper renovation and ratification of the covenant of grace; and no other wise. And those that take and eat and drink the sacramental elements at the Lord's Table with any other meaning, I fear, know not what they do.'[7]

This conviction led him to reject Stoddard's practice as 'wrong, and that he could not retain the practice with a good conscience. He was fully convinced that to be a visible Christian, was to put on the visibility or appearance of a real Christian; that a profession of Christianity was a profession of that wherein real Christianity consists; and therefore that no person, who rejected Christ in his heart, could make such a profession consistently with the truth. And as the ordinance of the Lord's Supper was instituted for none but visible professing Christians, that none but those who are real Christians have a right, in the sight of God, to come to that ordinance; and, consequently, that none ought to be admitted thereto, who do not make a profession of real Christianity, and so can be received, in a judgement of charity, as the true friends of Jesus Christ.'[8]

This caused uproar in the church and some members sought to have him removed from the pastorate. So that they could properly understand his position and calmly consider the issue, Edwards wrote for the study of church members, *An Humble Inquiry into the Rules of the Word of God, concerning the Qualifications requisite to a Complete Standing and Full Communion in the Visible Christian Church*. Apparently few members read it, so Edwards sought permission from the church officers to preach on the subject, but this was denied him. The end result of this sorry affair was that this godly man was dismissed from the pastorate. The whole text of *An Humble Inquiry...* is available to us today in the *Works of Jonathan Edwards* and will help us to see the thinking of Edwards and the vast amount of Scripture he gathers to prove his case.[9]

A sense of wonder

It may not be possible ever to ensure that we have a completely pure Lord's Supper regularly in our churches, but that should not stop us desiring and working towards that end. But this should never become our chief preoccupation. We must avoid the danger of so hedging the Lord's Table around that we forget what it is really all about. Too much regulation will distract our attention from its central message and solid comforts, both of which reside in the glorious person and saving work of Christ. As we come to the table our thoughts should not be over-burdened as to whether or not an unbeliever is present. Rather, our hearts should be overflowing with love and gratitude for the Saviour who loved us and gave himself for us. Christ should fill our hearts and minds as we take the bread and wine. Charles Wesley's sense of wonder should be ours:

> Died he for me, who caused his pain?
> For me, who him to death pursued?
> Amazing love! how can it be
> That thou, my God, should'st die for me?[10]

Notes

Chapter 1

1. From the hymn, 'The King of love my shepherd is' (*Grace Hymns,* no. 774).

2. John Calvin, *Institutes of the Christian Religion,* James Clark, 1953, vol. 2, p.491.

3. James Montgomery Boice, *Foundations of the Christian Faith,* IVP, 1986, p.595.

4. E. Kevan, *The Lord's Supper,* Evangelical Press, p.19.

Chapter 2

1. Kevan, *The Lord's Supper,* p.33.

2. As above, p.34.

3. Louis Berkhof, *Systematic Theology,* Banner of Truth Trust, 1959, p.298.

4. James Montgomery Boice, *Genesis,* Ministry Resources Library, 1982, vol. 1, p.256.

5. Leon Morris, *The Atonement,* IVP, 1983, p.22.

6. Kevan, *The Lord's Supper,* p.37.

7. From the hymn, 'My hope is built on nothing less...' by Edward Mote (*Grace Hymns,* no. 776).

8. From the hymn by Nicolaus von Zinzendorf (*Grace Hymns*, no. 792).

Chapter 3

1. Quoted by L. Boettner, *Roman Catholicism,* Banner of Truth Trust, 1966, pp.219-20.

2. Boettner, *Roman Catholicism,* p.252.

3. Berkhof, *Systematic Theology,* p.652.

4. Quoted by Boice, *Foundations of the Christian Faith,* p.604.

5. From the hymn, 'O Christ, what burdens bowed thy head!' by Anne R. Cousin (*Grace Hymns,* no. 493).

Chapter 4

1. J. C. Ryle, *Practical Religion,* James Clark, 1959, p.109.

Chapter 5

1. *Calvin's Commentaries,* Baker Book House, 1979, vol. 14, p.102.

2. As above, p.104.

Chapter 6

1. C. Hodge, *1 Corinthians,* Banner of Truth Trust, 1958, p.231.

2. C. H. Spurgeon, *The Gospel of the Kingdom,* Passmore & Alabaster, 1893, p.153.

Chapter 7

1. A. W. Tozer, *Man the Dwelling-Place of God,* Christian Publications, 1966, p.74.

2. Kevan, *The Lord's Supper,* p.49.

3. Ryle, *Practical Religion,* p.107.

Chapter 8

1. Ryle, *Practical Religion,* p.106.

2. As above.

3. John Brown, *Discourses and Sayings of our Lord,* Banner of Truth Trust, 1967, vol. 2, p.419.

4. Leon Morris, *Luke,* Tyndale New Testament commentaries, IVP, 1988, p.335.

5. Brown, *Discourses and Sayings,* p.429.

6. *The Works of Jonathan Edwards,* Banner of Truth Trust, 1976, vol .1, p.115.

7. As above, p.459.

8. As above, p.115.

9. As above, p.434.

10. From the hymn, 'And can it be...?' by Charles Wesley (*Grace Hymns,* no. 566).